Monitoring Western Snowy Plovers at Point Reyes National Seashore, Marin County, California

2011 Annual Report

Natural Resource Technical Report NPS/SFAN/NRTR—2012/645

Lacey Hughey

National Park Service
Point Reyes National Seashore
1 Bear Valley Road
Point Reyes Station, CA 94956

December 2012

U.S. Department of the Interior
National Park Service
Natural Resource Stewardship and Science
Fort Collins, Colorado

The National Park Service, Natural Resource Stewardship and Science office in Fort Collins, Colorado, publishes a range of reports that address natural resource topics. These reports are of interest and applicability to a broad audience in the National Park Service and others in natural resource management, including scientists, conservation and environmental constituencies, and the public.

The Natural Resource Technical Report Series is used to disseminate results of scientific studies in the physical, biological, and social sciences for both the advancement of science and the achievement of the National Park Service mission. The series provides contributors with a forum for displaying comprehensive data that are often deleted from journals because of page limitations.

All manuscripts in the series receive the appropriate level of peer review to ensure that the information is scientifically credible, technically accurate, appropriately written for the intended audience, and designed and published in a professional manner.

This report received formal peer review by subject-matter experts who were not directly involved in the collection, analysis, or reporting of the data, and whose background and expertise put them on par technically and scientifically with the authors of the information.

Views, statements, findings, conclusions, recommendations, and data in this report do not necessarily reflect views and policies of the National Park Service, U.S. Department of the Interior. Mention of trade names or commercial products does not constitute endorsement or recommendation for use by the U.S. Government.

This report is available from (http://www.nature.nps.gov/im/units/sfan) and the Natural Resource Publications Management website (http://www.nature.nps.gov/publications/nrpm/).

Please cite this publication as:

NPS 612/117777, December 2012

Contents

Contents (continued)

Figures

Tables

Appendices

Abstract

This report details the results of the 22nd year of the western snowy plover (*Charadrius alexandrinus nivosus*) monitoring program within Point Reyes National Seashore, Marin County, California (PRNS). The goal of the 2011 monitoring effort was to determine abundance, distribution, and breeding success of snowy plovers nesting on federal lands within PRNS. The report provides an overview of the 2011 snowy plover monitoring program on federal lands and summarizes the results of the data collected during the field season.

In 2011, there were 133 complete surveys conducted between Kehoe Beach and North Beach parking lot, eight from North Beach parking lot to the Lighthouse, 20 on Limantour Spit, and one on Drake's Spit to determine abundance and distribution of breeding snowy plovers. A minimum estimate of 14 plovers bred on Point Reyes National Seashore. Exclosures were placed around 13 of 15 nests located in 2011. Thirteen of 15 nests hatched at least one egg and 36 of 45 total eggs hatched. Eleven of 36 chicks survived for at least 28 days after hatching for a 31% fledging rate. The number of fledglings per egg was 0.24, compared to 0.17 in 2010 and an average of 0.3 since exclosures were first used in 1996. This season resulted in a better than average hatch rate and the highest number of chicks fledged since 2007, but the overall fledge rate remained well below average for the fifth year in a row.

Habitat restoration efforts continued throughout the season with the bulk of activity occurring January through July of this year. Over 190 acres of plover and rare plant habitat were restored after the mechanical removal of invasive European beachgrass (*Amophila arenaria*) near Abbott's Lagoon.

The Western Snowy Plover Docent Program remains an important tool to educate park visitors about the plight of the western snowy plover and to minimize potential negative impacts from visitors, especially those with dogs. Docents made 4,194 visitor contacts on weekends and holidays in 2011. The docent program should continue in future breeding season and a full-time seasonal docent coordinator is needed to recruit, organize, and lead the volunteer docents.

All efforts to improve habitat on all current and historic breeding beaches and reduce the impacts of human recreation and natural predators on nesting plovers should be continued and expanded at Point Reyes in order to reach the USFWS recovery goal of 64 breeding birds on Point Reyes beaches.

Acknowledgments

This project is made possible with funding from Point Reyes National Seashore, the National Park Service Youth-In-Parks Program, and the Point Reyes National Seashore Association. Protocol development is funded and supported by the San Francisco Bay Area Network Inventory and Monitoring Program.

Z. Green, R. James, L. Michl, M. Razi, S. Shpak, and D. Voeller, helped conduct surveys, provided transportation, and/or set up symbolic fencing and exclosures. Youth intern C. Campbell was irreplaceable in her role of field assistant and equipment manager. PRBO biologists L. Stenzel and G. Page were invaluable resources throughout the season and conducted additional surveys of Limantour Spit. Avocet Inc. biologists S. Bunnell, J. Evans, M. Flett, and J. Roth conducted additional nesting surveys during the Abbott's Lagoon Dune Restoration Project. PRNS staff N. Gates and D. Press provided technical supervision. PRNS volunteer docents logged 600 hours of volunteer time and contacted 4,194 visitors on weekends and holidays throughout the 2011 plover nesting season. None of these contacts would have been possible without the heroic efforts of J. Rolka and J. Wilkinson, who volunteered to carry out the duties of the Plover Docent Coordinator.

Introduction

In March 1993, the Pacific coast population of the western snowy plover (*Charadrius alexandrinus nivosus*) was listed as threatened by the U.S. Fish and Wildlife Service (USFWS). The population decline prompting listing was largely due to habitat degradation, predators, and recreational disturbance. In 1996, PRBO Conservation Science (PRBO) began helping the U. S. National Park Service reach the USFWS (2007) recovery goal of 64 breeding birds within Point Reyes National Seashore (PRNS) by recommending management actions and monitoring the birds' response to those actions. PRBO conducted intensive snowy plover research at PRNS for 18 years including 1977, 1986 to 1989, and 1995 to 2007. In 2008, Point Reyes National Seashore took over monitoring responsibilities for the breeding season (March-September) while PRBO continues to conduct the Winter Window Survey.

Annual breeding population sizes range from a high of 50 in 1987 to a low of 10 in 1996. Fledged chicks per egg rates (number of fledged chicks per egg) ranged from 0.01 in 1989 to 0.58 in 1996 and 1998. Nest failures have been largely attributed to predators and predator exclosures have been used by the park as a management tool since 1996. Beach visitors to PRNS have also been observed approaching active nests, which has been documented as a threat to nesting snowy plovers, especially when accompanied by a dog (Page et al. 1977). In response, the park established a snowy plover docent program in 2001 to educate beach visitors about the nesting snowy plovers and beach recreation restrictions.

Current monitoring objective

The overall goal of the western snowy plover monitoring program is to determine trends in the estimated breeding population size, distribution, and reproductive success of snowy plovers at known breeding beaches at PRNS.

Methods

Study Area

Snowy plovers have historically used Point Reyes Beach, Drake's Spit and Limantour Spit for nesting within Point Reyes National Seashore (Figure 1). Point Reyes Beach is separated into five beach survey areas: 1. Kehoe Beach entrance to Abbott's Lagoon (K); 2. Abbott's Lagoon (including the southwest shore of the lower pond of Abbott's Lagoon) to North Beach parking lot (NP); 3. The restored back dune habitat south of Abbott's Lagoon and adjacent to North Beach (RA) 4. North Beach parking lot to South Beach parking lot (NB); and 5. South Beach parking lot to Lighthouse Beach (SB). Limantour Spit (L) refers to the beach area from the Limantour Beach parking lot west to the end of Limantour Spit. Although Limantour has not been used by plovers during a breeding season since 2000, it continues to be surveyed. Drake's Spit (D) refers to the beach to the west side of the mouth to Drake's Estero (Figure 1).

On Kehoe (K) and North Beach (NP) sectors, there are two areas where European beach grass (*Ammophila arenaria*) was removed from 2004-2005. These sites and the additional snowy plover habitat they have provided are included in the respective sectors from 2004 to the present. An additional survey sector (RA) was created this season to encompass the habitat restored over the spring and summer of 2011. For more details on study area, see also Adams et al. (In review).

Heavy winter storms, particularly during ENSO (El Niño-Southern Oscillation) years, can significantly alter beach profiles at high-energy beaches such as at Point Reyes (White and Allen 1999). ENSO years may also result in more rain during the spring, at the start of the snowy plover breeding season. These combined negative impacts resulted in a 10 to 30 percent rangewide decline in the western snowy plover breeding population following the ENSO winter of 1997/1998 (USFWS 2007). For this reason, ENSO predictions from NOAA/National Weather Service are considered during our monitoring seasons at Point Reyes and in reporting our annual data.

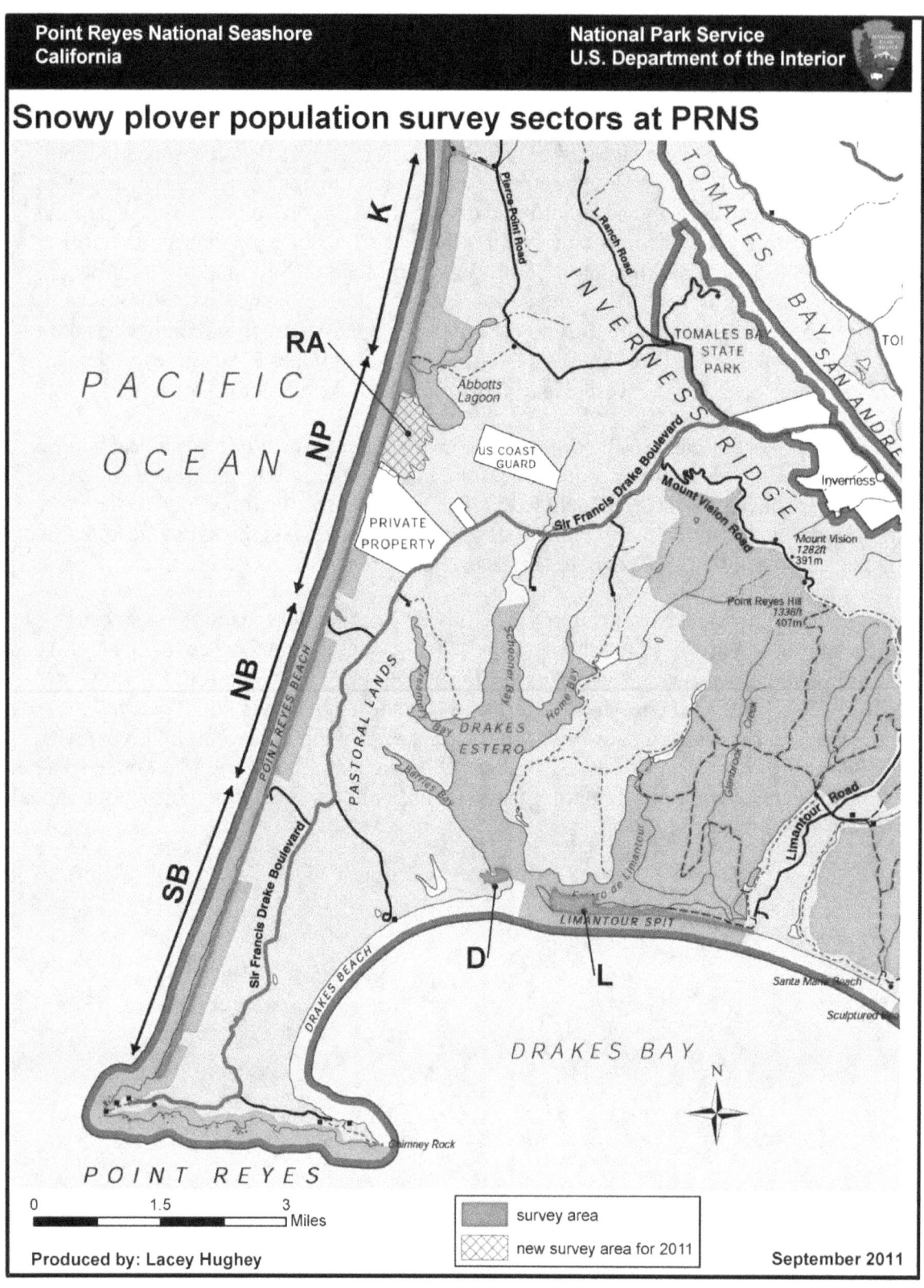

Figure 1. Locations of monitoring sectors, including: Kehoe Beach entrance to Abbott's Lagoon (K); Abbott's Lagoon to North Beach parking lot (NP); 2011 Abbott's Lagoon Dune Restoration Project Area (RA); North Beach parking lot to South Beach parking lot (NB); South Beach parking lot to Lighthouse Beach (SB), Limantour Spit (L), and Drake's Spit (D).

4

Field surveys

Breeding season surveys begin March 15th and continue until all broods have fledged in mid-September. Since breeding has recently been restricted to Kehoe Beach and North Beach, these sites are each surveyed at least twice a week. Limantour Beach is surveyed twice a month, though this season it was surveyed twice a week from late March-Mid June to assess the presence of nesting plovers. Drake's Beach, NB sector, and South Beach are each surveyed twice per season. The back-dunes along the southwest shore of Abbott's Lagoon are surveyed approximately two times per week in conjunction with the North Beach survey sector, though the frequency of surveys in this area may need to be adjusted based on future observations of plovers in this newly restored area.

The Winter Window Survey is the only survey conducted outside of the breeding season. During this survey, all current and historic plover breeding beaches are surveyed, range-wide, within a one week time frame. PRBO biologists have historically conducted this survey for all Point Reyes beaches (NP, NB, SB, K, L, and D survey sectors).

During surveys, observers walk just below the high tide line, crossing above the line only when necessary to see the full width of the beach. Observers stop every 50 to 100 m as necessary to scan up to 100 m ahead for plovers. When a plover is located, observers may approach as close as 10 m to determine age, sex, and color band combination if bands are present, though this is rarely done unless the adult is already standing and not involved in any nest building, incubating, or brood tending activities. Date, location (by GPS coordinates), and the time of sighting are recorded on datasheets. Observers then walk around the bird(s) to prevent flushing. Upon return to the office, all data is entered into a Microsoft Access Database.

Nest searching

Nests are located using three methods: 1) systematically searching microhabitats in which plovers are likely to nest; 2) watching potential breeding adults from a concealed position; and 3) following plover footprints in fine sand (Adams et al., In review). Once a nest is located, it is exclosed with a 10-foot by 10-foot square fence as soon as possible unless it is determined that high tide will threaten the nest. The two-inch × four-inch fence openings allow entrance and departure of plovers while keeping out mammalian predators. On the top of the exclosures, mesh netting is used to prevent access by avian predators. Exclosures are removed from the beach after the chicks have hatched and left the nest. The UTM coordinates of all nests are determined using GPS units and maps are produced at the end of each season (Appendix E).

Nests are checked two to four times per week to verify if they are still active. If a nest is not active during a particular visit, then cause of loss is determined using the criteria outlined in Appendix A. If a nest is abandoned by the adult plovers or has failed to hatch in over 35 days, the plover biologist will collect the unhatched eggs. The eggs are stored in a freezer at PRNS with the collection information until they can be transferred to an appropriate facility for methyl mercury and/or fertility testing (Miles et al. 2009). If a nest remains active through its projected hatching date, checks are made more frequently at that time to determine the precise hatch day.

Adults and chicks are searched for on follow up visits; once found, the number of chicks and location are recorded. If chicks are determined to be lost, then the criteria outlined in Appendix B are used to determine timing and cause of loss. If chicks survive 28 days after hatching, then they are considered fledged and are no longer monitored.

Predator counts

Native predators, particularly common ravens (*Corvus corax*), are a leading cause of chick and nest loss at Point Reyes National Seashore, so frequent population surveys are conducted to monitor changes in local population and distribution near plover habitat. Surveys are conducted in conjunction with daily plover surveys. All predators are recorded as they pass observers at a 90° angle on the beach or up to 75 meters into the dunes. Predators that flush in any direction from a stationary position in response to observers are also counted. However, predators that pass the observer and then immediately reverse direction are not counted. A GPS is used to record location of the observer when he/she is adjacent to the location of the predator at first sighting. Results are entered in a Microsoft Access Database.

Minimum population estimate

Due to the small plover population size at PRNS, it is possible to obtain an accurate estimate of the minimum population size without banding. A minimum population estimate is determined using the steps outlined in Appendix D and corroborated with the results of the annual, statewide Breeding Bird Window Survey. This survey involves surveying all current and historic breeding sites within the seashore during a pre-defined time period that's predicted to coincide with the peak of nesting season. Since Point Reyes typically observes peak nesting outside this time period, Appendix D is used to obtain a more accurate minimum estimate.

Western snowy plover docent program

In an effort to educate park visitors about the plight of the western snowy plover and to minimize potential negative impacts from visitors, especially those with dogs, the Western Snowy Plover Docent Program was established in 2001. Volunteer docents are stationed at trailheads leading to snowy plover habitat on all weekends and holidays between Memorial Day and Labor Day. Docents educate visitors about the plight of the snowy plover and the entire coastal dune ecosystem through one-on-one contacts, educational flyers, and guided observations of snowy plovers on the beach. Docents also serve an important role in addressing and reporting law enforcement violations conducted in and near snowy plover habitat.

The snowy plover docents are typically led by a full-time seasonal Park Guide to assist with organization and supervision of the group. This was the first season since the program began that the Park Guide position was not filled, so much of the Guide's duties were assumed by the docents and the Biological Technician.

Results

Number of surveys

During the 2011 plover breeding season (March 7th-September 22nd), there were 133 surveys conducted between Kehoe Beach and North Beach parking lot, eight from North Beach parking lot to the Lighthouse, 20 on Limantour Spit, and one on Drakes Spit to determine abundance and distribution of breeding snowy plovers. This compares to 150 surveys between Kehoe Beach and North Beach parking lot (K, NP), three from North Beach parking lot to the Lighthouse (NB, SB), eight on Limantour Spit (L), and two on Drakes Spit (D) in 2010.

Number of nesting plovers and nests

A minimum estimate of 14 plovers bred in Point Reyes National Seashore in 2011 (nine males, five females, Appendix D). This compares to a minimum estimate of 14 plovers (seven males, seven females) as derived from the Breeding Bird Window Survey this season. In 2010, there were also 14 breeding plovers at PRNS, compared to a total of 24 plovers that bred here in 2009 (Table 1, Figure 2).

Maximum numbers have not been reported since 2009 due to variability in observer detection and the adoption of a new methodology to determine the number of nesting plovers at PRNS (Appendix D). See Adams et al. for an explanation of methodology used to determine minimum and maximum numbers before 2009.

For the first time since exclosures have been used at PRNS, an incidental take occurred when an adult female became entangled in the netting used to cover the top of the exclosure placed around her nest (K02_2011). The associated male incubated the clutch for six days before all three eggs successfully hatched and eventually fledged two chicks.

Additionally, an intact and emaciated snowy plover carcass was recovered from the shore of Abbott's Lagoon and submitted for necropsy at the National Wildlife Health Center. There was no evidence of injury to the bird observed on necropsy. Although the bird was emaciated, heavy metal loads were all within normal ranges and both infectious disease and parasitology tests were negative. The cause of death for this snowy plover remains unknown.

Table 1. Number of western snowy plovers nesting at PRNS from 1986 – 2011.

Year	Females	Males	Total[1]
1986	22-23	19-21	41-44
1987	25-26	25-28	50-54
1988	21-22	19-20	40-42
1989	18-20	16-17	34-37
NO DATA	–	–	–
1995	6	6	12
1996	5-6	5	10-11
1997	12	13	25
1998	7	9	16
1999	9	11	20
2000	17-18	14-19	31-37
2001	13-19	14-17	27-36
2002	17-19	17-18	34-37
2003	11-12	12-13	23-25
2004	17-18	17-18	34-36
2005	9-10	10-11	19-21
2006	14-15	16-17	30-32
2007	14-15	16-17	30-32
2008	11-12	12-13	23-24
2009[1]	11	13	24
2010	6	8	14
2011	5	9	14

[1]In 2009, alternative methodology was developed to determine the number of nesting plovers at PRNS. See Appendix D for further explanation.

Red font signifies an ENSO event during June-November of that year.

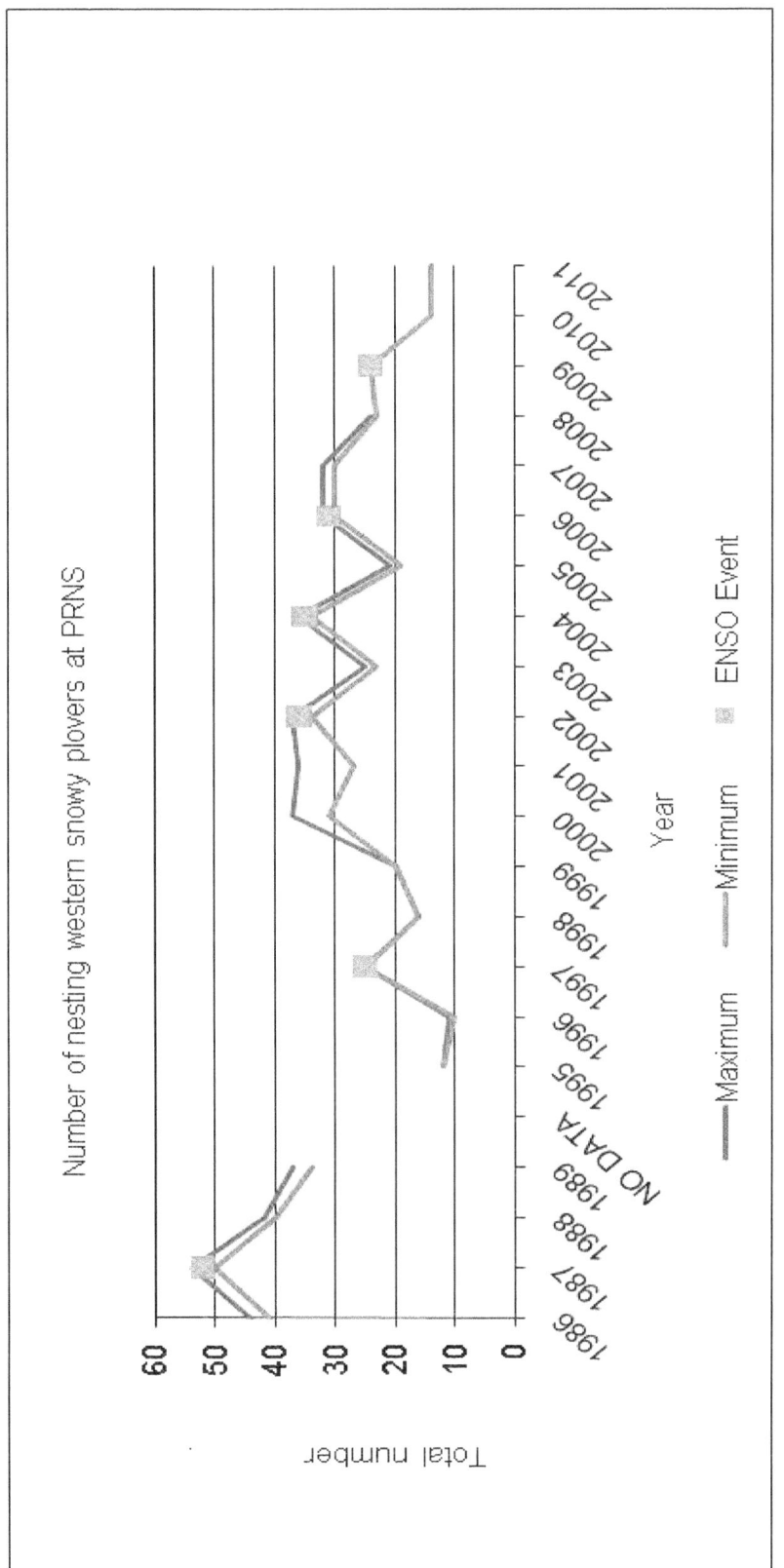

*ENSO event occurring between June and November of specified year.

Figure 2. Number of nesting western snowy plovers at PRNS and occurrence of El Niño (ENSO) events from 1986 – 2011.

9

Of the 15 nests located in 2011, 12 were between Abbott's Lagoon and North Beach parking lot and three between the Kehoe Beach entrance and Abbott's Lagoon (Appendix E). For the 11th consecutive year, no nests were found on Limantour Spit (Table 2). The hardpan area immediately north of the North Beach parking lot was used by nesting plovers for the third year in a row.

Table 2. Number of western snowy plover nests at PRNS, by survey sector, from 1986 – 2011.

Year	K	NP	NB	SB	L	Total
			Number of nests by beach survey sector[1]			
1986	5	29	1	2	4	41
1987	9	48	6	11	1	75
1988	5	41	7	12	0	65
1989	6	42	7	6	0	61
NO DATA	–	–	–	–	–	–
1995	4	11	5	0	0	20
1996	0	8	0	0	1	9
1997	0	18	0	0	7	25
1998	2	10	0	0	2	14
1999	0	16	0	0	5	21
2000	10	15	0	0	3	28
2001	8	26	0	0	0	34
2002	6	24	0	0	0	30
2003	6	16	0	0	0	22
2004	21	16	0	0	0	37
2005	4	15	0	0	0	19
2006	11	13	0	0	0	24
2007	14	14	0	0	0	28
2008	11	10	0	0	0	21
2009	9	12	0	0	0	21
2010	7	8	0	0	0	15
2011	3	12	0	0	0	15
[2]Mean	7	15	0	0	1	23

[1]K = Kehoe Beach to Abbott's Lagoon

NP = Abbott's Lagoon to North Beach parking lot

NB = North Beach parking lot to South Beach parking lot

SB = South Beach parking lot to Lighthouse Beach

L = Limantour Spit

[2]Mean is from years with exclosures (1996-2011).

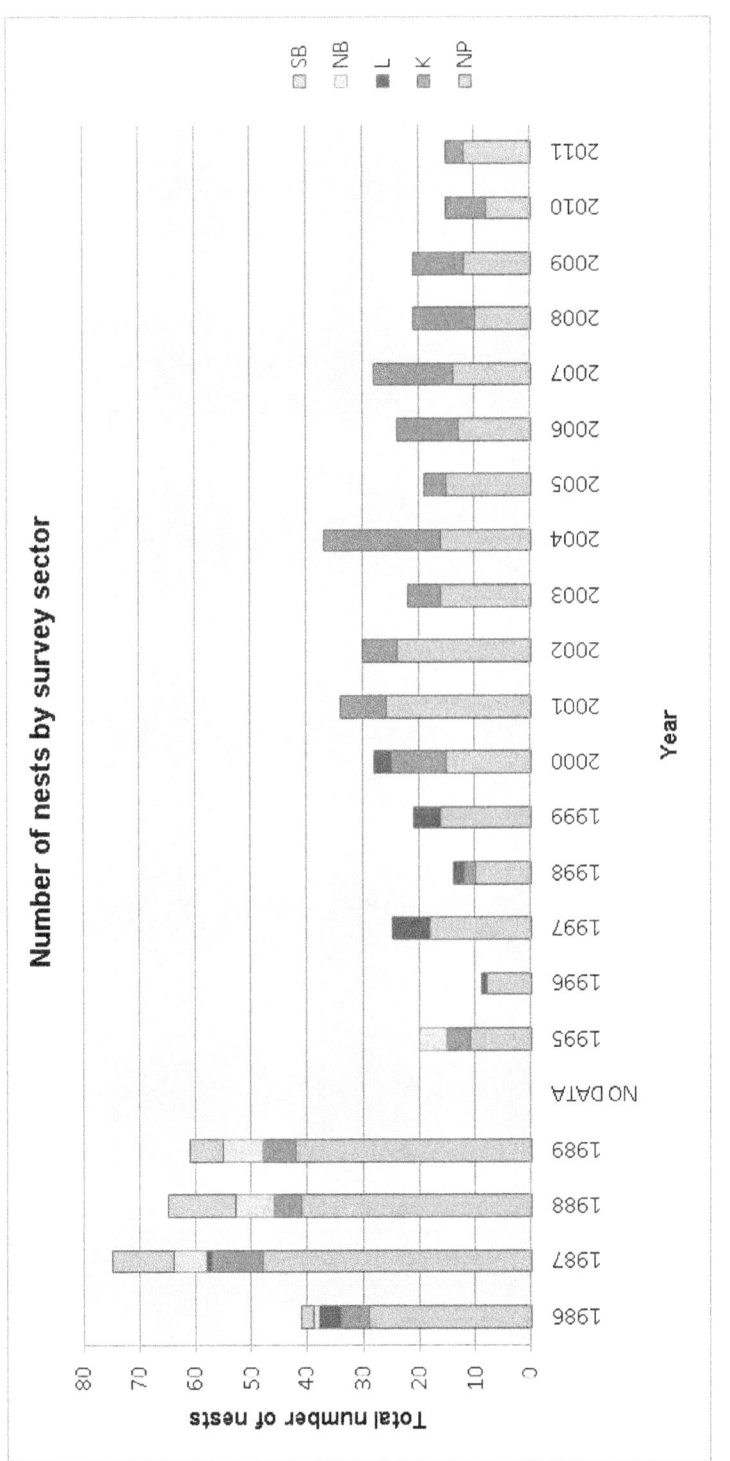

K = Kehoe Beach to Abbott's Lagoon

NP = Abbott's Lagoon to North Beach parking lot

NB = North Beach parking lot to South Beach parking lot

SB = South Beach parking lot to Lighthouse Beach

L = Limantour Spit

Figure 3. Number of western snowy plover nests at all surveyed beaches from 1986 – 2011.

Nest success

Exclosures were placed around 13 of the 15 nests in 2011. Overall, 13 of 15 nests hatched at least one egg and 36 of 45 eggs hatched (Table 3, Figure 4). Of the nests that failed to hatch, one was not exclosed due to its position under a large log. The cause of loss for this nest could not be determined (Table 4). The other failed nest was exclosed and was abandoned following a possible depredation event of one of the incubating adults (Figure 5). The carcass of the adult was never recovered but the disturbance evidence inside the exclosure suggested depredation by weasel.

See Appendix A for an explanation of criteria used to determine nest loss and Appendix C for details on the fate of all nests found in 2011.

Table 3. Western snowy plover nest success on Point Reyes Beach from 1986 – 2011. Includes Kehoe (K) and North Beach (NP) survey sectors only.

	Nests		Eggs			Chicks		
Year	Number	% Hatched	Number	Number Hatched	% Hatched	Number Fledged	% Fledged	Fledged Per Egg
1986	35[1]	31.4	99	31	31.3	8	25.8	0.08
1987	74	19.0	198	35	17.7	15	42.9	0.08
1988	65	7.7	161	11	6.8	5	45.5	0.03
1989	61	1.6	146	3	2.1	1	33.3	0.01
NO DATA	–	–	–	–	–	–	–	–
1995	20	10.0	55	5	9.1	4	80.0	0.07
1996	8	75.0	24	16	66.7	14	87.5	0.58
1997	18	72.2	44	33	75.0	20	60.6	0.45
1998	12	100.0	36	35	97.2	21	60.0	0.58
1999	16	87.5	47	39[2]	83.0	22	56.4	0.47
2000	25	56.0	72[3]	41	57.3	14	34.1	0.20
2001	34	26.5	86[4]	25	29.1	10	40.0	0.12
2002	30	50.0	76	41	53.9	17	41.5	0.22
2003	22	77.2	63	43	68.3	19	44.2	0.30
2004	37	78.3	107	86	80.4	19	22.1	0.18
2005	19	63.1	53	33	62.3	17	51.5	0.32
2006	24	79.2	69	51	73.9	23	45.0	0.33
2007	28	82.1	83	64	77.1	24	37.5	0.29
2008	21	52.3	55	30	54.5	5	16.1	0.09
2009	21	66.7	60	38	63.3	8	21.0	0.13
2010	15	60.0	42	21	50.0	7	33.3	0.17
2011	15	86.7	45	36	80.0	11	30.5	0.24
[5]Mean	22	68.4	61	40	66.1	16	44	0.30

[1] 37 nests were located in 1986 but only 35 were monitored for success.
[2] 38-40 eggs hatched
[3] 71-72 eggs laid
[4] 85-87 eggs laid
[5] Mean includes data from first year exclosures were used in 1996 through 2011.

12

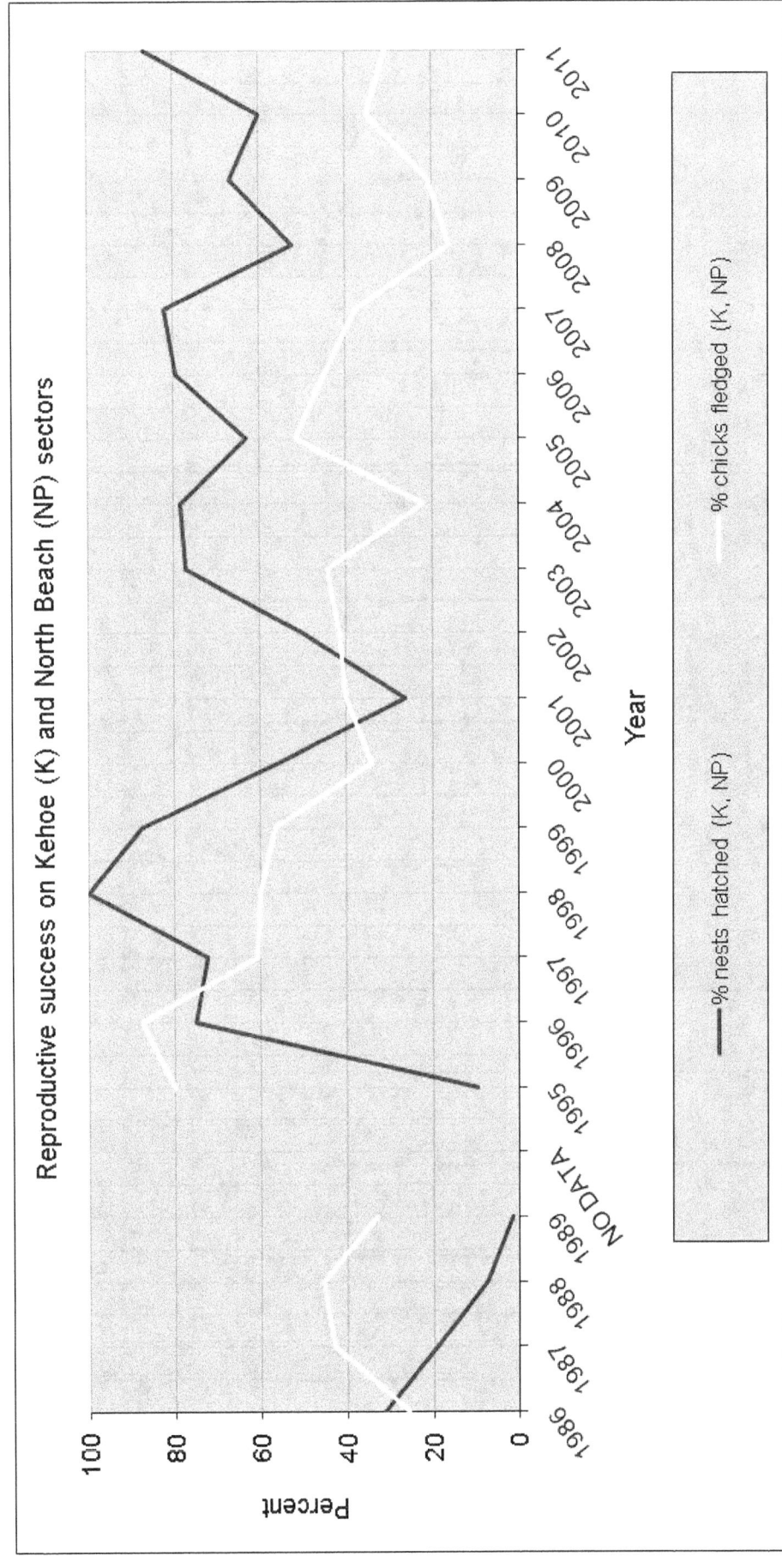

Figure 4. Comparison of reproductive success parameters on Point Reyes Beach (K, NP) from 1986 – 2011.

Table 4. Causes of western snowy plover complete nest loss on Point Reyes Beach (includes Kehoe (K) and North Beach (NP) survey sectors).

Year	Total Nests	Nests Exclosed	Raven		Wild Canid[1]		Bob-cat		Other Predator[2]		Unidentified Predator		Unknown		Abandon-ment		Environ-mental[3]		Unhatched Eggs	
			N	E	N	E	N	E	N	E	N	E	N	E	N	E	N	E	N	E
1996	8	7	1													1				
1997	18	13	3								2									
1998	12	12																		
1999	16	16						1												4
2000	25	25										1		5			1	1		
2001	34	16	11		2					1	2	1	1	8	1	1	2	1		
2002	30	20	5		1					1	2			3	2	2	1		
2003	22	22												2			3		
2004	37	32			1								1	1		5		
2005	19	16			2	1							2	2	2			
2006	24	23				1								2				2
2007	28	22	1								3					1		
2008	21	18	2								3					5		
2009	21	19	1							1	1	1				3		
2010	15	15												3				
2011	15	13									1			1				1

N = Nest was not exclosed

E = Nest was exclosed

[1] "Wild Canid" includes coyotes and foxes

[2] "Other Predator" includes other avian species and rodents

[3] "Environmental" includes wind and tides

14

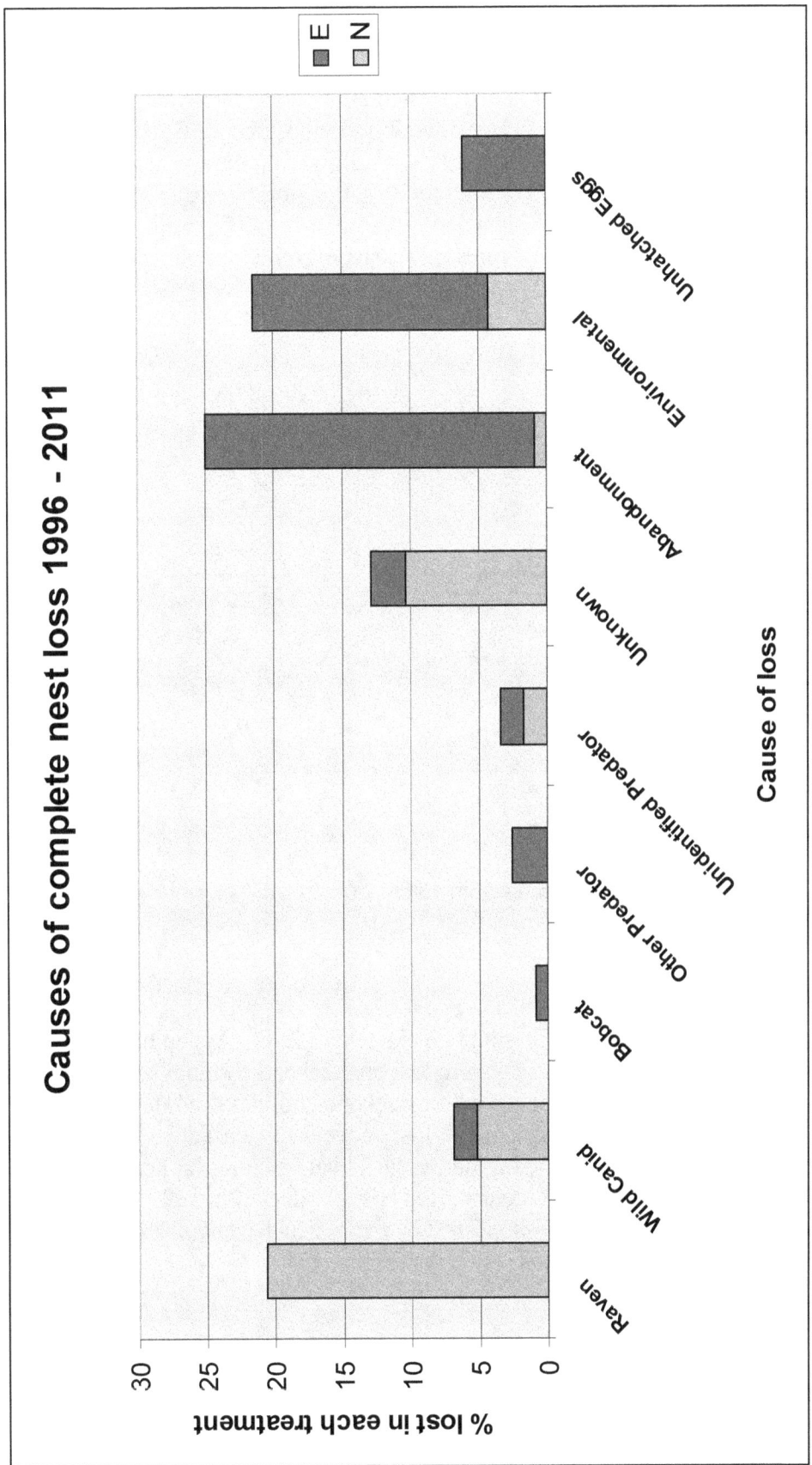

Figure 5. Percent of total nests lost for exclosed nests (E) and non-exclosed nests (N) from 1996 – 2011.

Fledging success

Eleven of 36 chicks survived to fledging (for at least 28 days) after hatching, a 30.5% fledging rate (Table 3). Of the estimated nine breeding males in 2011, seven successfully fledged one or more chicks (78%) compared to 75% in 2010 and 38% in 2009. One chick was fledged from the hardpan area immediately north of the North Beach parking lot (Appendix E). One chick was fledged from this area in 2010 and two chicks in 2009, which was the first year snowy plovers were recorded using this area for nesting. Overall, the 2011 fledging rate was at least 1.2 chicks per male, the first time a rate above 1.0 has been achieved since 2007 (Figure 6). The USFWS has set a recovery goal of maintaining fledge rates of at least one chick per male to attain a sustainable population (USFWS 2001).

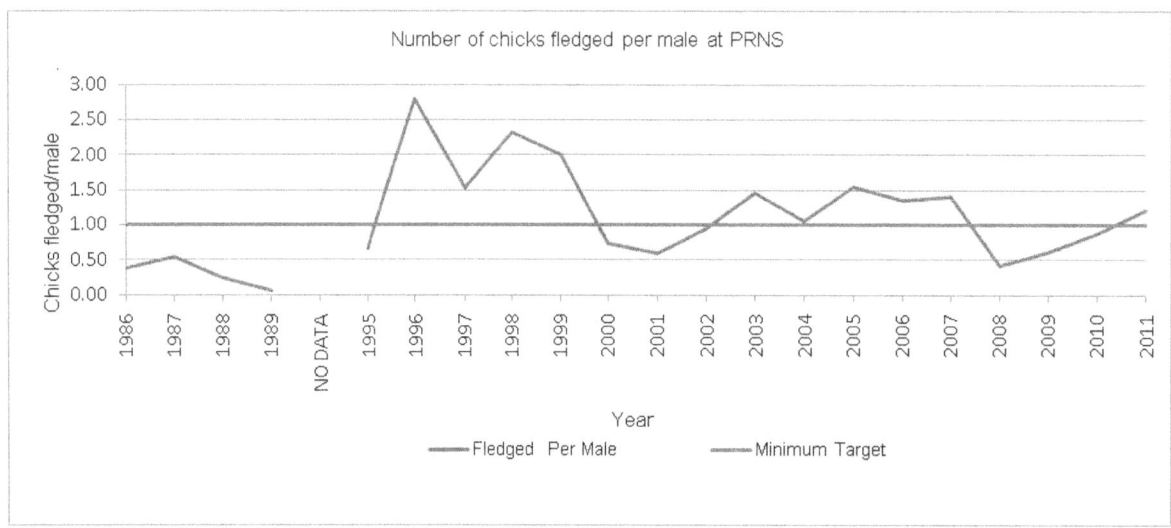

Figure 6. Total number of chicks fledged per male from 1986 – 2011.

Timing of chick loss

The timing of chick loss was determined for all 25 chicks lost in 2011 (Appendix B). Of the 18 chicks that failed to fledge on North Beach, 14 were lost on weekends/holidays, and four on weekdays. On Kehoe Beach, three losses occurred on weekends/holidays, while four losses occurred on weekdays. Overall, 68% of chicks were lost on weekends/holidays, which constituted 42% of all days that chicks were on the beach. This is the highest percentage of chicks lost on weekends and holidays since data started being collected in 1999 (Figure 7). In 2011, 86% of chicks that failed to fledge disappeared by the age of 10 days, 14% from ages 11-20 days, and no chicks were lost from ages 21-28 days (Figure 8).

Figure 7. Percent of pre-fledge chicks lost on weekends/holidays from 1999 – 2011.

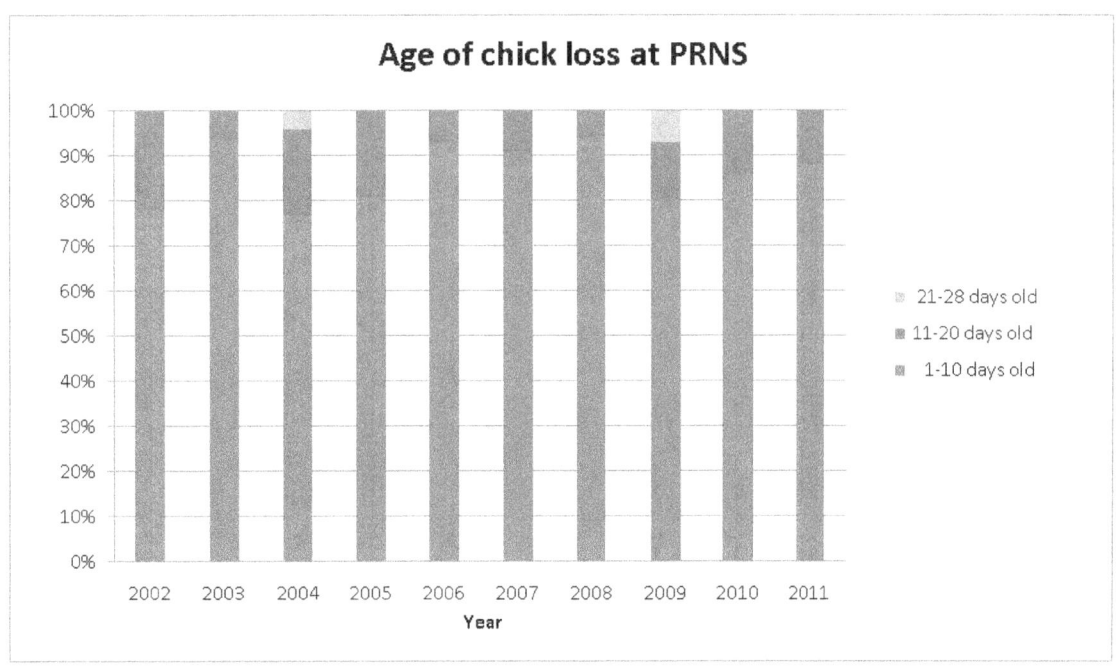

Figure 8. Percent of chicks lost in each age category from 2002 – 2011.

Plover use of restored habitat

Though *Ammophila arenaria* was removed from two areas on NP and K sectors in 2004 and 2005, only the restored area on Kehoe (K) has been maintained over time. Thus, *A. arenaria* on North Beach (NP) has returned to pre-restoration levels, making assessment of use of this "restored" habitat of limited value for this area. Therefore, we only report data for the area restored in 2004 and 2005 for the Kehoe sector. However, additional habitat was restored in NP this season (RA sector, Figure 1), which will also be shown here. It should also be noted that excavation of *A. arenaria* was occurring in this area through July 2011, so nesting this season may have been discouraged by such activity.

Of three nests on Kehoe Beach, two were on the beach adjacent to the *A. arenaria*-covered dunes. The location of the third nest could not be determined because it was not discovered until the brood of chicks was present on the beach. Of 12 nests on North Beach, one was located in the foredunes of the recently restored area.

No chicks were fledged from restored areas on Kehoe in 2011. Three chicks from a single brood were fledged from the restored area adjacent to NP and two chicks from two different broods successfully fledged after frequent utilization of the northern and southern edges of the restoration area.

Raven occurrence

Common ravens (*Corvus corax*) have been a constant presence on Point Reyes beaches since monitoring began in 2002. On Kehoe Beach in 2011, ravens were detected on 65% of surveys, averaging 3.3 birds per survey hour. This compares to 81% of surveys and an average of 2.9 birds per survey hour in 2010, and 98% of surveys and an average of 4.1 birds per survey hour in 2009 (Figure 9, Table 5). On North Beach in 2011, ravens were detected on 50% of surveys, averaging 0.77 birds per survey hour. In comparison, ravens were detected on 62% of surveys averaging 0.94 birds per survey hour in 2010 and 67% of surveys, averaging 0.98 birds per survey hour in 2009 (Figure 9, Table 5).

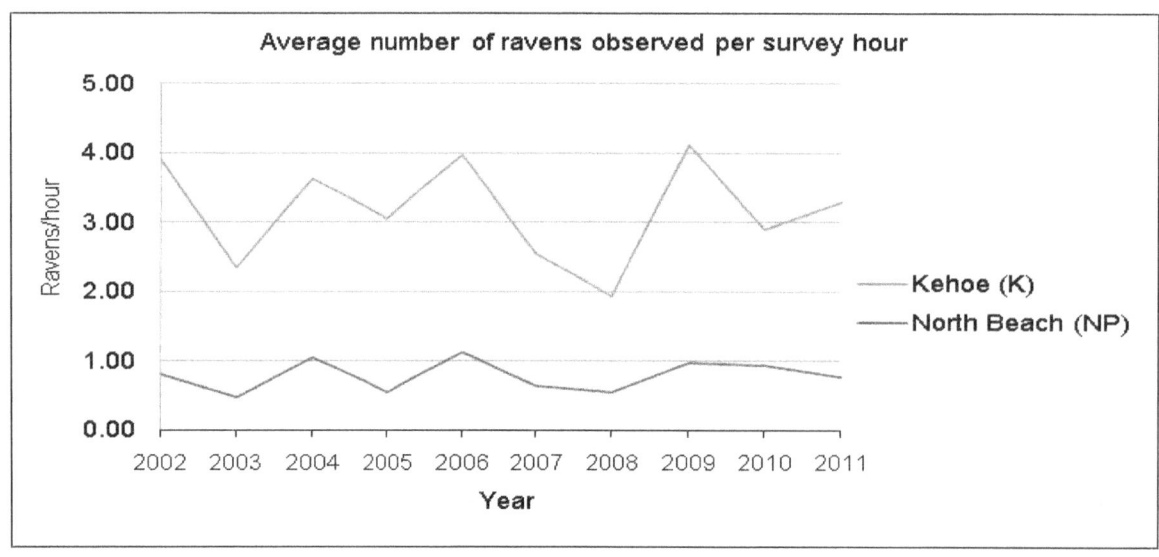

Figure 9. Average number of ravens observed per survey hour from 2002 – 2011.

Table 5. Occurrence of common ravens on surveys from 2002 – 2011.

Year	No. of Surveys	Total Survey Hours	Surveys with Ravens	Total Raven Sightings	% Surveys with Ravens	Average Ravens per Survey	Average Ravens per Survey per Hour
Kehoe (K)							
2002	47	120	39	470	83	10.0	3.91
2003	41	128	22	300	54	7.3	2.34
2004	72	292	66	1062	92	14.8	3.64
2005	40	95	34	291	85	7.3	3.05
2006	76	211	68	836	89	11.0	3.97
2007	78	312	71	795	91	10.2	2.55
2008	86	344	64	666	74	7.7	1.94
2009	50	125	49	512	98	10.2	4.11
2010	68	132	55	449	81	8.0	2.90
2011	57	125	37	412	65	7.2	3.3
Average	**62**	**188**	**51**	**579**	**81**	**9.4**	**3.17**
North Beach (NP)							
2002	57	172	31	141	54	2.5	0.82
2003	72	231	20	108	28	1.5	0.47
2004	62	150	25	158	40	2.6	1.06
2005	68	121	18	65	27	1.0	0.54
2006	76	204	48	230	63	3.0	1.13
2007	70	350	68	228	97	3.3	0.65
2008	61	305	45	169	74	2.8	0.55
2009	45	165	30	194	67	4.2	0.98
2010	58	143	36	160	62	4.0	0.94
2011	64	199	32	154	50	2.4	0.77
Average	**63**	**204**	**35**	**161**	**56.2**	**2.7**	**0.79**

Discussion

Number of nesting plovers

The minimum estimate of 14 nesting snowy plovers on Point Reyes National Seashore in 2011 compares with a mean of 24.0 (SD = 7.2) individuals in the 14-year period from 1996 to 2010, during which exclosures have been used to protect nests. This ties with 2010 as the lowest estimated minimum number of nesting plovers since 1996 (Table 1). This low number of adults could be related to the low number of fledglings from Point Reyes in the past three years, which could reduce the number of returning nesting adults for this season.

Additionally, the possible impacts of El Niño (ENSO) winter storm events continue to be considered since the resultant beach erosion could be a contributing factor in reducing available nesting habitat. It may also affect over winter survival rates of potential breeding adults, thus causing a decline in breeding population the following summer. The winter of 2010-2011 was not classified as an El Niño event and the population has remained stable from 2010 to 2011. Alternatively, Figure 2 shows a recurring pattern of decreased total number of breeders in years following ENSO events. This trend would support the need for large scale habitat restoration at Point Reyes and further investigation into the impacts of climate change on western snowy plovers.

Two adult female snowy plover carcasses were recovered this season. One was the result of an incidental take due to entanglement in the netting used to cover the top of an exclosure. This female was apparently flushed abruptly from her nest on Kehoe Beach by an unknown disturbance and became entangled in the netting in the process. Human, canine, and corvid tracks were found around the nest site, though the nest was located over one mile from the nearest trailhead and visitors were rarely observed in this area on surveys. The netting used on this exclosure was particularly taught and additional supports had been used on the exclosure walls to reduce flexibility of the structure. After a review of the incident, USFWS determined that no changes in exclosure protocol were necessary since such an event has never been recorded in the 16-year history of exclosure use at Point Reyes and it was highly unlikely to occur again. The second female was found dead and emaciated during a routine nest check on the southwest shore of Abbott's Lagoon. This bird was unmarked and not associated with an active nest or brood at the time. The cause of death for this snowy plover remains unknown.

Nest hatching rate

The 86.7% clutch hatching rate in 2011 compares with a mean of 68.4% (SD = 17.9) from 1996-2010. Figure 4 shows that post-management hatch rates (1996-2011) have increased compared to pre-management hatch rates. This is likely due to the success of predator exclosures at protecting nests until hatch. However, post-management fledge rates have decreased compared to pre-management fledge rates, suggesting the need for further investigation into the causes of chick loss in future seasons.

Abandonment was the cause of one nest loss this season. Based on the evidence, a predator, believed to be a weasel because of the round rodent sized tracks found inside the exclosure, appears to have entered the exclosure and depredated the incubating adult. The eggs were intact, but rolled out of the scrape in the direction of the prevailing wind and a few feathers were located around the exclosure.

Abandonment was the primary cause of nest lost in 2010 (20% lost) and a recurring cause of nest loss from 2000 to 2006. However, no nests were lost to abandonment from 2007-2009. The reasons for most of the recorded abandonment events are unknown, but the relationship between prolonged exclosure use and increased adult mortality rates (Neumann et al. 2004) has been documented on several other beaches and prompted an internal review of exclosure use at Point Reyes. The conclusions of this review suggested that predation pressures on unprotected nests at Point Reyes are too high to warrant a reduction in exclosure use. However, cases of nest abandonment will continue to be closely investigated and the use of exclosures will be re-evaluated on a yearly basis.

Chick fledging rate

In 2011, the 30.5% fledging rate at Point Reyes was lower than the 43.5% (SD=18.4) average of the previous 15 years (Table 3). However, the rate has climbed steadily since falling to an all-time low in 2008 (16.1%).

The USFWS uses the chick fledgling rate to gauge progress towards a sustainable coastal population of western snowy plovers, and aims to have at least one chick fledged per male in order to achieve this goal (USFWS 2001). From 1995 to 2007, the Great Beach (SB, NB, NP, and K combined) at Point Reyes surpassed that goal by producing an average of 1.42 chicks per male. However, in 2008, only 0.42 chicks were fledged per male due to unknown reasons. Since 2008, number of chicks per male has steadily increased and this was the first season more than one chick was fledged per male since 2007 (Figure 6).

Timing of chick loss

As in the past seven years, most chick losses occurred during the first third of the fledging period (88%) (Figure 8). Though chicks as old as 21-28 days old have been lost in the past, no chicks were lost in that age group this year. The largest percentage (68%) of chicks were lost on weekends and holidays versus weekdays this year compared to all previous years this metric has been recorded (33% average since 1999, Figure 7).

Weekend and holiday chick loss declined dramatically in years following the implementation of the docent program in 2003. These levels have remained relatively steady since then and there is not a clear explanation for the increase to 68% in losses observed this year. Though the docent program was greatly reduced in scope this season, 4,194 visitor contacts were made in 2011, which is comparable to previous years, and it is not likely that this alone could account for the great increase in weekend losses. It is possible that the difference could be an artifact of reduced brood checks due to the increased demand for surveys in the RA sector and Limantour spit. Reduced brood checks resulted in reduced accuracy of timing of chick loss data collected.

Of the chicks lost on weekends between 2009 and 2011, a greater proportion has been lost on North Beach (82%) versus Kehoe Beach (18%). Since the portion of North Beach used by nesting plovers is much closer to areas of high visitation than Kehoe Beach, it is possible that human (and dog) presence continues to be a significant factor in young chick mortality. Therefore, increased law enforcement beach patrols, clear and durable signage, public outreach as well as a strong docent presence at trailheads and on beaches are continued priorities for the plover management program.

Use of restored dune habitat

Snowy plovers were documented using restored dune habitat for the ninth consecutive year. Though *Ammophila arenaria* has returned to pre-restoration levels in the dunes south of Abbott's Lagoon (in sector NP), the dunes north of Abbott's Lagoon (in sector K) have been maintained to prevent encroachment of *A. arenaria*. Additionally, 180 acres of habitat were restored in NP this season (sector RA, Figure 1). Therefore, we will only report data for the area restored north of Abbott's Lagoon in the Kehoe sector and will begin reporting data for sector RA. It should also be noted that excavation of *A. arenaria* was occurring in sector RA through July 2011, so nesting this season may have been discouraged by such activity.

No nests were initiated in the restored dunes of sector K this season. Despite extensive efforts to reduce human disturbance through symbolic fencing, signage, and the docent program, no nests have ever been established in this area since its restoration in 2005. However, wintering groups are frequently sighted feeding and roosting in this area during early and late nesting season and several nests have been established adjacent to this site, though none this year.

The lack of nesting in this portion of restored habitat may be attributed to the consistent presence of large groups of ravens that roost on the hill adjacent to this site. Previous attempts to deter ravens from this area included use of bald eagle decoys, hazing, and lethal removal of territorial pairs. While bald eagle decoys and hazing were not used this year, lethal removal was employed as a means of reducing corvid impacts to plovers in this area.

Of the 12 nests on North Beach (NP), one was located in the foredunes adjacent to the recently restored area (RA). Though not technically inside the restoration project area, the adults and chicks of this nest likely benefited from their proximity to the improved habitat of sector RA. This was the first nest in three years to fledge all three chicks and the brood was frequently sighted feeding and roosting within the boundaries of RA.

Additionally, two other broods from nearby nests were observed utilizing the northern and southern boundaries of sector RA on multiple occasions. These broods each fledged one chick. When combined with the three fledges mentioned above, fledges occurring within RA accounted for 46% of all fledges from Point Reyes this season.

Due to various set-backs in the early stages of the 2011 dune restoration project, heavy equipment and multiple field crews operated daily in sector RA through mid-July of this season. The impact this may have had on nesting plovers in this area is not known, but it should be noted that a nest did occur in the restored area once all heavy equipment had been removed from the foredunes.

Raven occurrence

The number of ravens observed per survey hour on Kehoe (3.30) and North Beach (0.77) in 2011 was close to average (3.20, 0.78 respectively) for the 10 years ravens have been monitored at PRNS (Table 5, Figure 9). Fifty-seven surveys were conducted for ravens on Kehoe Beach in 2011 and ravens were present on 65% of those surveys. On North Beach, where ravens have historically been seen in comparatively lower numbers, they were detected on 50% of surveys; the lowest percentage since 2005. No nests loses could be attributed to ravens in 2011 (Table 4).

Lethal removal was used as a predator management strategy for corvids for the seventh year in a row at PRNS. When used in combination with non-lethal predator control strategies, targeted removal of territorial pairs has been shown to have a "...large, positive effect on hatching success of the target bird species..." (Cote' et al 1997). Removal at Point Reyes targeted only those corvids either identified as responsible for depredation of snowy plovers or observed actively hunting in snowy plover nesting areas.

Vandalism

Since 2008, occurrences of vandalism have remained relatively infrequent. There have been up to three instances of vandalism per year since 2008. This season, all three instances involved removal of pet restriction signage installed at Kehoe Beach. Law enforcement surveillance and re-installation of vandal proof signs along the Kehoe trail eliminated vandalism activities in this area for the rest of the season. This compares to 19 instances of vandalism in 2007 and 24 in 2006. The dramatic decrease in vandalism may be largely attributed to the placement of permanent "No Dogs" signs along Kehoe Trail and at the entrance to the beach from North Beach parking lot. This signage has likely communicated a more official message than the temporary signage used in the past and is likely more difficult to vandalize than the laminated signs on wooden posts that were easily removed and vandalized in the past.

Although biologists, park employees, and docents were present on the beaches during busy weekend times, human footprints were still seen inside symbolic fencing and leading up to exclosures, especially near nests visible from the area of Abbott's Lagoon.

Research activities and recommendations

Continue current monitoring

It is critical that PRNS continue monitoring the breeding population of snowy plovers at Point Reyes. The Recovery Plan (USFWS 2007) sets a goal of 50 adult birds on Point Reyes Beach (K, NP, NB, and SB; there were 14 in 2011), ten on Limantour Spit (L; there were zero in 2011), and four on Drakes Spit (D; there were zero in 2011). The plan also recommends that a reproductive rate of one fledged chick per male is the minimum required to sustain the population (2011 rate was 1.22 chicks per male, Figure 6).

Continued monitoring will help to determine if these population goals are being met and allow managers to respond to new and increasing threats in a timely manner. Implementation of a banding program may be an important step in achieving these goals by offering insight into survivorship rates, site fidelity and improving the quality of data collected at PRNS.

It may also be important to analyze historic nesting data with regards to efficacy of exclosures at increasing fledgling survival. Recent reports from Oregon suggest that exclosure use may increase hatch and fledge success up to the first several years of use, but that over time, increasing adult and chick depredation events near exclosures may actually decrease fledge success (Lauten et al. 2010). Due to the observed decrease in fledgling success since 2008, evaluation of past and future exclosure use is warranted. The implementation of a banding program will assist in determining if exclosures are associated with adult depredation in PRNS.

Predator data collection and analysis

Improved methods for predator data collection were tested in 2011 in response to peer review criticisms to the draft monitoring protocol (Adams et al., In review). The current methods were not considered adequately systematic or standardized to assess how fluctuations in predator abundance, especially common ravens, affect snowy plover nest success and productivity. The draft methods tested this season better quantify the time spent searching for predators and utilize a line transect method for collecting predator data. Using distance sampling techniques (Buckland et al. 1993), the data should allow for calculations of predator abundance and density that can assessed in regards to the recovery of snowy plovers at Point Reyes. These methods should be further refined in the next breeding season(s), be peer-reviewed, and formally incorporated into the snowy plover monitoring protocol.

In the future, predator monitoring data should be assessed for correlations with land management practices at the local and regional scale. For example, any seasonal trends across the plover breeding season that correlate with nearby agricultural activities are important to document. Subsidized feeding from dairy operations is a likely cause of raven increases in the Point Reyes area in the past decade (Kelly and Etienne 2002).

Peregrines may also be an important plover predator and a pair was first observed nesting and feeding in the historic plover nesting area around Abbott's Lagoon in 2009. They were observed less frequently in this area in 2010 with resurgence in peregrine activity occurring in 2011. Peregrines were observed on approximately 5% of surveys in both 2009 and 2010 and 16% of surveys in 2011. No instances of depredation on snowy plovers were recorded, but the likelihood of detecting such an event is low. Thus, further monitoring of peregrines is warranted in order to monitor and mitigate impacts to nesting plovers in this area. Monitoring the effects of bald eagle decoys and effigies is also recommended to determine efficacy of such methods.

Project staff

Interns and volunteers provide invaluable assistance in the field, so efforts to recruit and compensate them should be continued and expanded. Hiring a part-time, seasonal field monitoring intern provides the added benefit of a trained and skilled observer. Since 2010, the intern has been included in the USFWS Threatened and Endangered Species Permit, which enabled the field team to conduct surveys on multiple beaches in the same day and allowed data to be collected in the absence of the lead biologist. Efforts should continue to be made at the beginning of each season to include the intern on the monitoring permit.

Since monitoring plovers requires a significant amount of training to become familiar with field techniques, the program would greatly benefit from retaining the same field technician from year to year. If this is infeasible, at least one field season of full time snowy plover monitoring should be a prerequisite for employment.

Education and outreach

The educational and informational visitor contacts on weekends and holidays by park employees and volunteer docents appears to be effective in increasing understanding and compliance of habitat closures. One measure of success is the 27% decrease in average percent chick loss over weekends and holidays that has been observed since the docent program started in 2003 (Figure 7). Although weekend/holiday chick loss in 2010 fell well below average, with only 21.4% lost, the percentage spiked in 2011 to 68%. Since it is difficult to isolate the reason for the fluctuation in weekend/holiday chick loss, continued beach patrols by law enforcement rangers and stationing of park interpretive employees and docents at trailheads is still recommended.

Management activities and recommendations

Habitat restoration

The 2004 to 2007 breeding seasons indicated that the removal of beach grass has a positive effect on the raising of plover chicks. Data from these seasons shows increasing numbers of nests and chicks being reared in these areas immediately following removal of European beach grass. The high proportion of fledges from sector RA in 2011 further supports the eradication of invasive dune grass from PRNS.

However, the lack of plover activity in the restored dunes of sector K and the unmaintained dunes of sector NP from 2004 to 2007, also emphasizes the range of variables that must be considered in any habitat restoration endeavor. Thus, appropriations for predator management and weed maintenance of restored sites should continue to be made in order to maximize benefits from the initial restoration effort.

Predator management

To attain a sustainable plover population, predator management recommendations are outlined below. Where feasible, the effectiveness of all implemented management actions should be assessed through monitoring.

- implementation of agricultural operation Best Management Practices (covering feeding troughs)

- reducing, over time, silage harvesting in fields adjacent to plover breeding areas and rescheduling remaining silage harvesting to reduce attraction of ravens during plover breeding season

- enforcing current restrictions on dairy ranch permittees concerning disposal of cow carcasses and afterbirths, thus reducing food subsidization of corvids

- managing "problem" ravens (i.e. ravens seen attacking plovers or nests, or perching regularly near nests or broods) throughout the breeding season, but especially within the first month of the season (April)

- focusing avian predator management efforts in dune restoration areas

- continue testing use of bald eagle decoys and, where appropriate, raven effigies, in strategic locations along the dunes, to deter patrolling by avian predators

- further reduce *Ammophila arenaria* coverage (dune restoration) within plover breeding habitat to reduce cover for terrestrial predators.

Visitor education and restrictions

The Point Reyes Plover Docent Program continues to be a key element for successful protection of breeding plovers. In addition to continuing the program, the park should consider extending the docent season to include the month prior to nesting (March) and the month of September until all chicks are fledged. This could reduce disturbance to early nesting pairs that initiate courtship up to 30 days before actually laying a nest (USFWS 2001) and contribute to increased fledging success for late season nesters.

It is also highly recommended that a full-time seasonal docent coordinator be on staff to recruit, organize, and lead the volunteer docents. This was the first season that the coordinator position was not filled and the pitfalls of this approach became strikingly clear. Though the volunteers were willing to take on many of the responsibilities of the coordinator, the lack of a designated leader ultimately resulted in confusion and frustration for the group. Additionally, without a coordinator, we could not recruit or train new volunteers to ensure the future of a program that already depends on a relatively small number of volunteers.

Literature Cited

Adams, D., M. Koenen, K. Peterlein, D. Press, and S. G. Allen. In review. Snowy plover monitoring protocol for Point Reyes National Seashore. Natural Resource Report. National Park Service, Fort Collins, Colorado.

Buckland, S. T., Anderson, D. R. Anderson, K. P. Burnham, and J. L. Laake, J. L. 1993. Distance sampling: estimating abundance of biological populations. Chapman and Hall, London. 446 pp.

Cote', I. M., and W. J. Sutherland. 1997. The effectiveness of removing predators to protect bird populations. Conservation Biology 11(2): 395-405.

Kelly, J. P., K. L. Etienne, and J. E. Roth. 2002. Abundance and distribution of the common raven and American crow in the San Francisco Bay area, California. Western Birds 33: 202–217.

Lauten, D. J., K. A. Castelein, J. D. Farrar, A. A. Kotaich, and E. P. Gaines. 2010. The Distribution and Reproductive Success of the Western Snowy Plover Along the Oregon Coast – 2009. Unpublished report for the Oregon Department of Fish and Wildlife – Nongame Program, Portland, the Coos Bay District Bureau of Land Management, Coos Bay, and the Dunes Recreational Area, Reedsport. The Oregon Biodiversity Information Center, Portland State University/INR, Portland, Oregon.

Miles, A. K., M. A. Ricca, and S. E. Spring. 2009. Snowy plovers at Point Reyes National Seashore: unraveling the mystery of mercury. Unpubl. Data Summary, U.S. Geological Survey, Davis, California. 49 pp.

Neuman, K. K., G. W. Page, L. E. Stenzel, J. C. Warriner, and J. S. Warriner. 2004. Effect of mammalian predator management on snowy plover breeding success. Waterbirds 27(3): 257-376.

Page, G. W., J. S. Warriner, J. C. Warriner, and R. M. Halbeisen. 1977. Status of the snowy plover on the northern California coast. Part I: Reproductive timing and success. California Department of Fish and Game Nongame Wildlife Investigations, Sacramento, CA. 6 pp.

U.S. Fish and Wildlife Service (USFWS). 2007. Recovery plan for the Pacific coast population of the western snowy plover (*Charadrius alexandrinus nivosus*). In 2 volumes. U.S. Fish and Wildlife Service, Sacramento, California.

U.S. Fish and Wildlife Service (USFWS). 2001. Western snowy plover (*Charadrius alexandrinus nivosus*) Pacific coast population draft recovery plan. U.S. Fish and Wildlife Service, Portland, Oregon.

White, J. D., and S. G. Allen. 1999. Draft western snowy plover management plan. Point Reyes National Seashore Unpublished Report, Point Reyes, CA.

Appendix A. Criteria and evidence for determining fate of snowy plover clutches.

Hatched

- Tapping or cracks observed in eggs one to two days before eggs disappeared – not fail safe.

- Eggs disappear close to estimated hatch date with no signs of predation

- Indication of a newly hatched brood in the immediate vicinity (direct observation, broody behavior exhibited by nearby adult).

- Flattened scrape with tiny egg shell fragments located in scrape.

Not hatched

Depredated - Unknown Predator:

- Direct evidence that eggs were destroyed, including:

  - Substrate cemented together by egg contents, or

  - Egg shell fragments intact but damaged eggs found well before estimated hatch date.

- Eggs gone well before estimated hatch date, no predator tracks to nest, but wind or tide would not have destroyed nest. Evidence may include:

  - Scrape intact or still discernible, or substrate stable or level enough such that wind would not cause clutch to be buried or eggs to roll out of scrape, or

  - Substrate too firm for imprint of predator tracks.

- Unidentified potential predator tracks directly to and at nest site (if potential predator tracks are observed leading towards nest site but gait is unchanging directly past nest site, that predator is not associated with clutch loss).

Depredated - Known Predator:

- Identified predator tracks directly to the nest site.

- Timing of lain predator tracks coincides with nest loss, as indicated by substrate conditions.

Tide:

- Tide has washed over the original nest location leaving no evidence of the eggs or nest scrape, and there is no indication of a newly hatched brood in the vicinity
- Eggs located near original location or nest washed over by the tide but no indication eggs being incubated.

- Tide has washed over nest location, eggs located near original nest location and being incubated well past estimated hatch date.

*Non-viable Eggs:
- Intact eggs of full clutch remain well after estimated hatch date along with evidence that there is consistent adult activity at nest location. Adult activity can be determined by presence of adult on nest, egg position changing from survey to survey. Nests should be monitored until adult activity ceases.

*Abandoned:
- Intact eggs of clutch remain but evidence of adult activity at nest ceased well before the estimated hatching date. No evidence nest was washed over by tides or ever buried by wind blown sand or other debris.

*Wind:
- Eggs not being incubated and one of the following:

    o Intact eggs located outside of scrape, eggs not being incubated, and no indication that any other species may have moved eggs, or

    o Eggs in scrape and covered by wind-blown sand or other debris.

*Note: Distinction between the above three categories (non-viable eggs, abandoned, and wind) can be difficult and may require additional information.

Trampled:
- Eggs found destroyed (not depredated) and tracks of a larger species directly through nest location.

Destroyed – Human:
- Human footprints directly next to or on the nest location and:

    o one or more eggs missing from the clutch, or

    o evidence that eggs were destroyed including shell fragments or contents.

- Human footprints near nest with evidence that something was dragged over, dropped or placed on nest.

Failed Unknown:
- Eggs gone well before estimated hatch date, but absence of clear evidence of depredation, wind loss, tide, or trampling.

Unknown:
- Eggs gone close to estimated hatch date, but evidence of hatch would have been obscured by weather conditions or other factors.

Appendix B. Criteria for determining snowy plover brood fate.

Determining hatch date:
- Make notes of when bird activity first started.

- When was the first egg laid?

- When was the clutch complete (usually 3-5 days)?

- Nests should be checked daily at 25 days past known clutch completion.

- If exact clutch completion date cannot be determined, nest checks should be made more frequently at 20 days past estimated completion. Your field notebook should provide good clues to bird activity around the nest site making it possible to closely estimate hatch dates.

Monitoring broods:
- Once a nest has hatched, chicks should be checked daily to determine timing of any loss that may occur.

- Approach the area where the brood was last seen slowly and cautiously.

- Are there adults present? And if so, are they displaying broody behavior (flying, vocalizing or feigning injury)?

- Can you easily see the chicks? Often, chicks are within a few meters of the adult.

- If a brood is located immediately, count the number of chicks present, location, and behavior. Record this information in your field notebook. Leave the area quickly, particularly if the tending adult is agitated.

- If the brood is not immediately located, move away to a concealed position and wait for the birds to resume undisturbed behavior. Again, count the number of chicks present, location, and behavior in your notebook.

- Once the brood is located and counted, leave the area. Any additional notes should be written well away from the site.

- If additional data collection is required (disturbance study or better aging) do so from a concealed area where your presence is not a factor and the birds are not disturbed further.

- First, determine what information is needed. For example, is it important to know the exact time of loss? Or, does general knowledge of loss suffice for your study area?

- When needing to determine the difference between weekday and weekend loss, all broods should be checked on Friday afternoon and again on Monday morning. If chicks are present on Friday but not on Monday morning, this is considered a weekend loss and should be recorded in your field notebook and data sheets as such.

- When trying to determine whether chick loss occurs in the day, at night, or at dusk or dawn, checks must be made within each of those time periods. For example, if chicks are present at 7 pm and at again at 9 pm, but not present at 5 am, the loss event would be recorded as occurring at night (take into consideration changing hours of sunrise and sunset).

- Determining the timing of chick loss events can be time consuming and somewhat difficult. Remember that most brood checks cause some disturbance to the birds and should only be done at a minimum frequency required to answer your research questions.

- If exact date of chick loss cannot be determined, the midpoint between 2 brood checks when a reduction in brood size is determined should be used as the date of loss.

Appendix C. Fate of snowy plover nests at PRNS in 2011.

Nest & Location[1]	Date Found	Exc.[2] Yes/No	Female ID[3]	Male ID[3]	Eggs Laid	Eggs Hatched	Clutch Fate	Final Status
NP01	4/18/2011	YES	U	U	3	3	HATCH	FLEDGE 0
NP02	4/25/2011	YES	U	U	3	3	HATCH	FLEDGE 0
NP03	5/9/2011	YES	w:av	U	3	3	HATCH	FLEDGE 1
NP04	5/23/2011	NO	U	U	3	0	FAIL	UNKNOWN
NP05	5/29/2011	YES	U	U	3	0	FAIL	ABANDONED
NP06	6/6/2011	YES	U	U	3	3	HATCH	FLEDGE 0
NP07	6/10/2011	YES	U	U	3	3	HATCH	FLEDGE 3
NP08	6/14/2011	YES	U	U	3	1	HATCH	FLEDGE 1
NP09	6/15/2011	YES	U	U	3	3	HATCH	FLEDGE 0
NP10	7/14/2011	YES	:Oy	U	3	3	HATCH	FLEDGE 1
NP11	7/17/2011	YES	U	U	3	2	HATCH	FLEDGE 1
NP12	8/5/2011	YES	U	U	3	3	HATCH	FLEDGE 2
K01	6/26/2011	YES	U	U	3	3	HATCH	FLEDGE 0
K02	7/3/2011	YES	U	U	3	3	HATCH	FLEDGE 2
K03[4]	7/27/2011	NO	U	U	3	3	HATCH	UNDETERMINED

[1]K = Kehoe Beach to Abbott's Lagoon; NP = Abbott's Lagoon to North Beach parking lot (including shore of the lagoon).

[2]Exc.=exclosure.

[3]U=unknown.

[4]K03 was discovered post-hatch as a brood of chicks. Date found represents date of first discovery of chicks. Final status is undetermined since age of chicks could not be confirmed and there was a low frequency of sightings for this brood.

Appendix D. Criteria for determining minimum numbers of western snowy plovers breeding at PRNS.

In 2009, it was determined that maximum estimates will no longer be appropriate due to the subjectivity involved in analyzing behavioral characteristics, as was required by the original methodology (Adams et al., In review). The advent of seasonally changing staff and a need for objective, repeatable methodology resulted in adoption of the following method for determining a minimum estimate:

1. Determine the time period when the maximum number of simultaneously active nests and broods were present on the beach during the breeding season and use data from this period to calculate the minimum number of breeders using the methods below:

    a. An active nest represents the presence of 1 male and 1 female (count = 1 male, 1 female).

    b. If one or more chicks of a brood are known to be alive and less than 3 weeks old, one male is inferred (count = 1 male).

    c. If a male is present with a brood greater than 3 weeks old, that male is probably with a new mate who may have initiated a new nest. This nest, if found, would result in counting of 1 male and 1 female. Therefore, males with broods of over 3 weeks are not counted (count = 0 male)

        i. However, if it is possible to determine that there are no available (unpaired) females within the vicinity, one male may be counted (count=1 male).

    d. One day prior to the estimated initiation date of a nest represents the presence of one male and one female which are about to nest (count=1 male, 1 female).

        i. This step is only relevant if a pair initiates a nest one day after the last day of the peak number of nests present on the beach.

    e. If any banded birds had confirmed nests outside of the peak window, add 1 male and 1 female (count = 1 male, 1 female).

Given the relatively small number of birds and few banded ones at PRNS, this method has been determined to be the best possible *minimum* estimate. However, years with a high rate of nest loss could result in inaccurate estimates since all of the birds won't have active nests. Therefore, results of the window survey for that year should also be reported as further corroboration of minimum numbers.

Appendix E. Western snowy plover nest locations at PRNS, April 2011-August 2011.

North Beach (NP) sector:

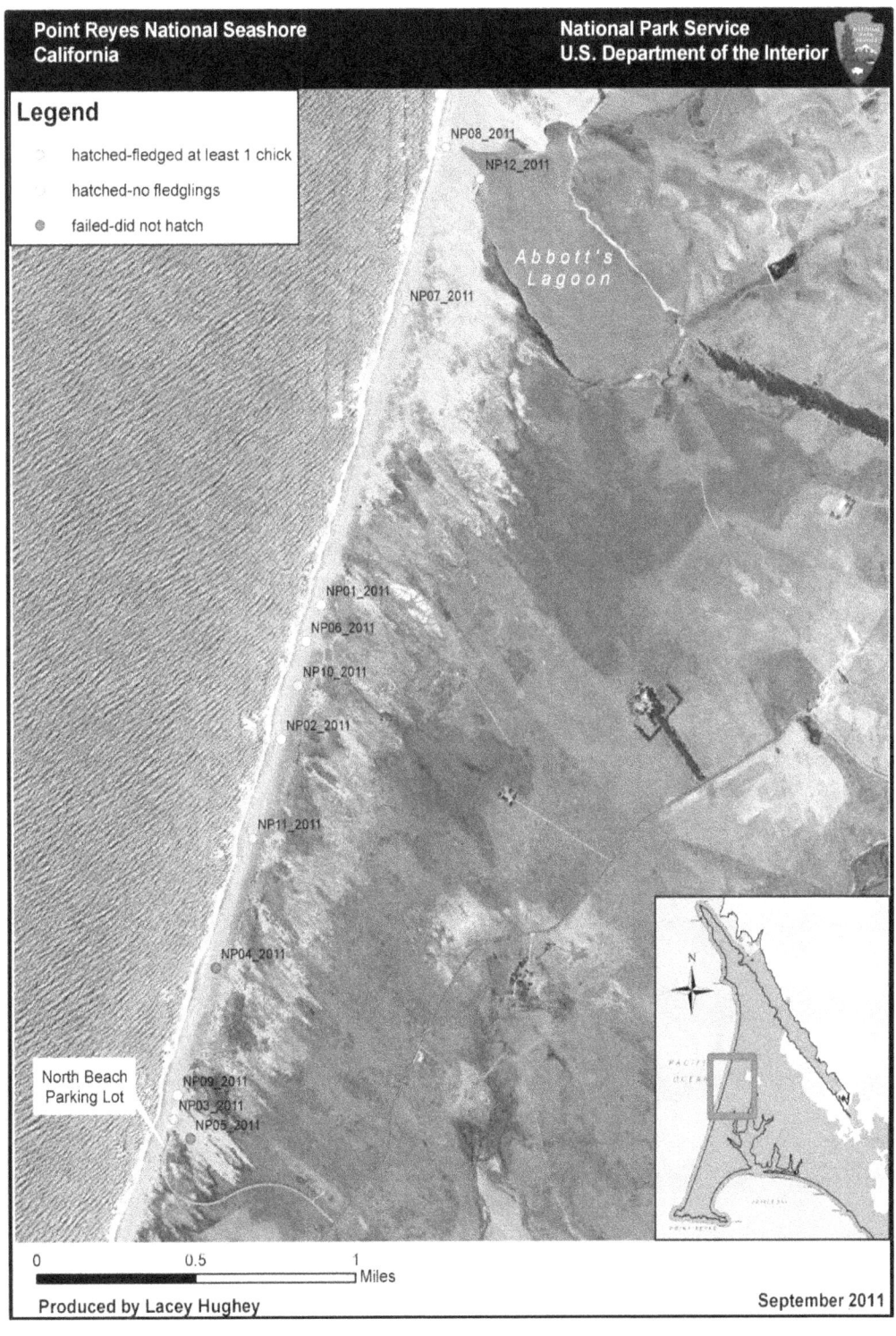

Kehoe (K) sector:

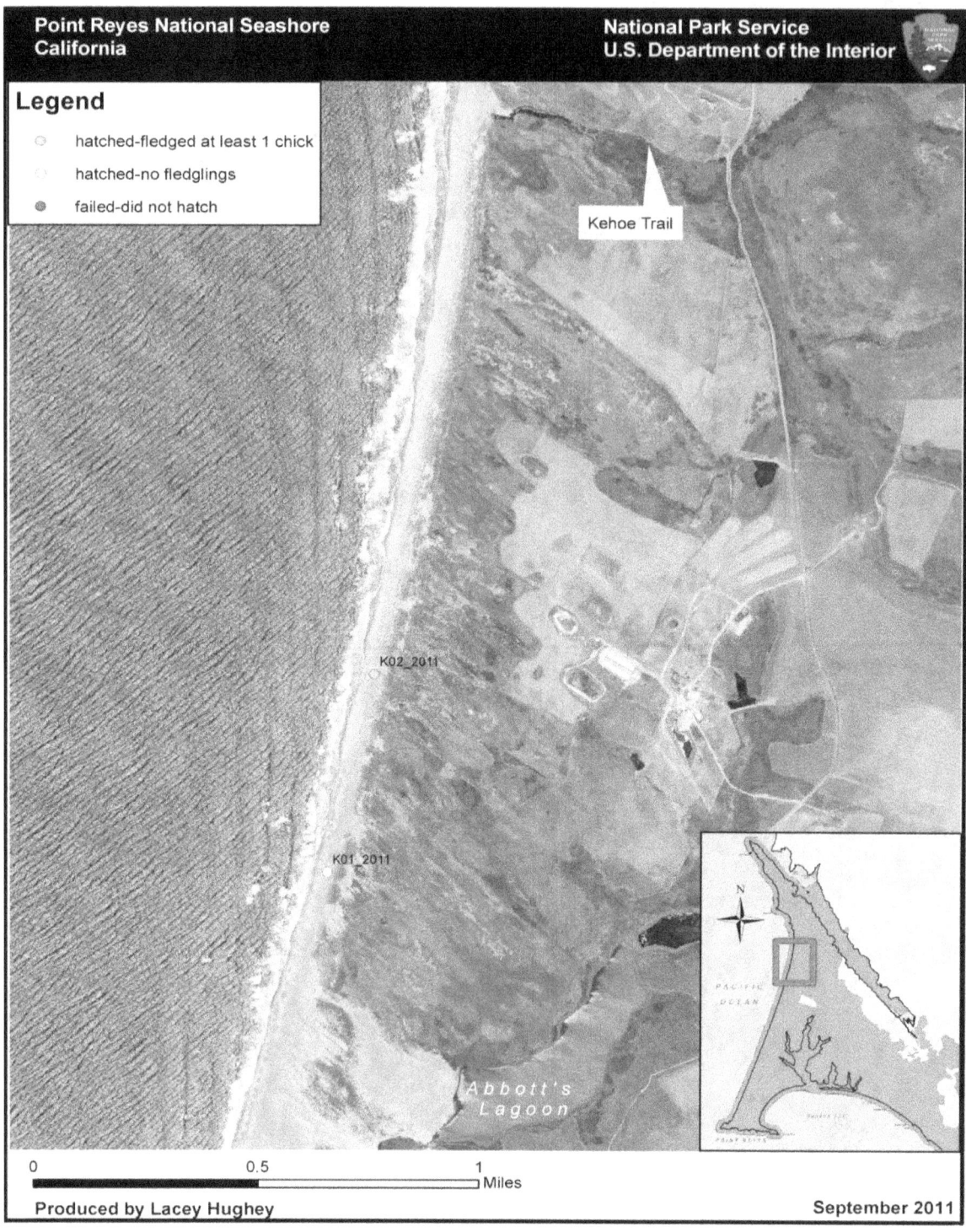

NPS 612/117777, December 2012

National Park Service
U.S. Department of the Interior

Natural Resource Stewardship and Science
1201 Oakridge Drive, Suite 150
Fort Collins, CO 80525

www.nature.nps.gov